Worton & Marston

A Community Remembers The Great War

Published by New Generation Publishing in 2019

First Edition

ISBN 978-1-78955-806-7

www.newgeneration-publishing.com

Credits

The contents of this book are a written and photographic record of the event.

The individual family histories were compiled by relatives or individuals who donated them for public display and study at the event and as a permanent record (this book). They appear in this book in no specific order or level of importance. All information was provided by individuals for the public to view at the event and in any permanent record made of the event. All the individuals who provided information or family records are responsible for the content and accuracy of that information. It was provided freely for the public to view and record. All artefacts, such as medals, documents, helmets, uniforms were photographed then returned to the owners at the end of the event. All photographs were taken at the public event in the full knowledge of those participating and attending.

We would like to thank the following people and organisations for their support and contributions to the event

Worton Rose and Crown Knit Natt Group:

Jo Banks, Val Dodd, Dot Francis, Rachael Ganuszko, Cheryl Hailstone, Chris Johnson, Jane Lovey, Sally Swanell, Alison Parker. Plus the many village volunteers who helped with knitting the poppies and erecting the Village Hall display.

People who contributed family records or artefacts for the event:

Robin & Judy Sherfcliff, Michael Stokes, David & Christine Johnson, Jan Rose, Brian Badge, Mark Fisher, Primrose Wright, Bryn Evans, Cheryl & Ian Hailstone, Alison Garside, Val & Rob Dodd, Dot Francis, Margaret Tucker, John Lane, Giles Collins, Paul Sperring, Andrew Stocks. Alison Parker, Dennis Brickley for his metal *There-but-not- There* soldier, Andy Kostyszyn, the Lansdown family and finally Paul Ganuszko for the slide presentation.

Worton Parish Council for its support and grant from the Solar Farm Fund**. The Royal British Legion. Worton Rose & Crown Public House and Wiltshire Radio.** Thank you for their support in helping to make the event so successful.

Proceeds from the sales of this publication will be split between Worton and Marston Village Hall and Christ Church Worton.

Chris and David Johnson

It was 100 years since the end of the Great War on November 11th 2018.

This is how the Worton and Marston community remembered

J. ELLIS
ROYAL NAVY

The Event

What a fantastic community event occurred in the Worton and Martson village hall. This event took over a year to organise. It began with the local ladies Knit Natt group deciding to knit 1,918 poppies, then gained growing local support until it culminated with organising a whole weekend event.

Firstly family histories, photographs and artefacts were requested from local families. There was an incredible response with over 30 family histories, many artefacts and volunteers to help during the event. The team became known as the *Poppy Crew*. Once the family histories were collated and mounted, a programme for the weekend event was produced. News of the proposed event spread and BBC radio Wiltshire came and interviewed the Poppy Crew.

The Poppy Crew also went to visit Five Lanes School to share the villagers' memories and to talk to the children about their own family histories. The children responded with great interest and a multitude of questions!

Next the village High Street was transformed by huge red poppies placed on the telegraph poles throughout the village. Many poppies were also displayed on villager's garden hedges. Finally the village hall was festooned in the 1,918 knitted poppies.

What a spectacular sight!!! Many, many passers-by and visitors drove through the village and stopped to take photographs.

Finally after over a year's work and planning the weekend arrived. It was an emotional weekend with over 600 visitors, many reading the display boards with tears in their eyes.

The artefact session was only planned to last one hour, however it proved so popular that it was extended to last all Saturday afternoon and all Sunday!

Sunday morning also saw a large gathering of villagers for a service of remembrance outside the village Hall, which then progressed to the nearby church.

Edwin John Burbidge

Edwin John (Eddie) Burbidge and his brother and sister were the three children of farm labourer John Burbidge and his wife Ellen who lived in the house next to today's *Mill Stream House* by the Bulkington Brook. He was baptized in Christ Church in October 1898. The family prospered in farming, moved to Close Farm in Marston (which burned down in 1956), and sent their two boys to the local school while their daughter went into service in Wingfield House near Trowbridge.

Edwin John Burbidge at War

Private Edwin Burbidge was conscripted in Devizes into the 1st Battalion Somerset Light Infantry. This (Prince Albert's) Regiment raised 17 Battalions, was awarded 60 Battle Honours and 1 Victoria Cross, and lost 4760 men during the course of the Great War.

He had just turned 18 when he arrived on the Western Front in France to join his Regiment which was part of the 11th Brigade in the 4th Division. They had already fought in the Battle of the Marne, the Battles of Aisne and Messines, the Second Battle of Ypres and the Battle of Albert.

With Burbidge in their ranks, the 1st Somersets went on to fight the Battle of Le Transloy in 1916 followed by the third Battle of the Scarpe, the great Battle of Polygon Wood, the Battle of Broodseinde, the Battle of Poelcapelle and the First Battle of Passchendaele in 1917. Then in 1918 they were in action in the First Battle of Arras, the Battle of Hazebrouck and the Battle of Bethune.

It was here in Bethune in Flanders that on Monday the 15th April 1918 the 1st Somersets were in the line at Riez du Vinage north of Bethune. It is likely that Edwin John was a member of the 1st Somerset's Light Company which took part in an attack on the German positions at the Bois de Pacaut at 5.40pm on that day. As the Light Company attacked they were met by hostile rifle and machine gun fire, and the remnants of the British attackers were forced to fall back. Edwin Burbidge was not among them.

Commemoration

Edwin was 19 years old at the time of his death; he has no known grave but, as well as in Christ Church Worton, he is remembered on the same memorial at Loos (Panel 38/39 in his case) as Herbert Alfred Dunford from *Sideways Cottage*.

As with most service personnel in the First World War, Edwin John Burbidge was posthumously awarded the Victory Medal and the British War Medal.

And After?

Father, Edwin John (senior), continued to farm until his death in 1944. *Close Farm* famously burned down in 1956 when pigs in the sty knocked over a paraffin heating lamp. His wife, Ellen, ran a village shop of sorts in *Close Farm* and when the house burned down she continued to do so from *Orchard View Cottage* (which is still there in Close Lane). Ellen died in 1948 and is buried with her husband in the Christ Church churchyard, where their tombstone also bears the memory of their 'son Eddie killed in action'.

Eddie's sister Mabel Ellen, having brought up her family in Yorkshire, returned here to lodge with her and Eddie's younger brother Frederick and his family in Manor Farm Potterne. Mabel's granddaughter still lives in Potterne

Frederick and his wife Dorothy (Few from West End Farm Marston) farmed Manor Farm in Potterne where they brought up their two daughters. Together with his wife, he is buried in Worton close to his parents where the grave is to this day tended by one of his granddaughters.

John Burbidge

The story of John Burbidge's short life is a sad one though no doubt one repeated many times throughout the country in the course of the Great War. His antecedents here in Worton went back to well before the French Revolution. However, winding the clock forward three generations from then, Frank Burbidge (an agricultural Labourer) and his wife Mary (Nutland from Littleton Panel) had eight children, all born in Worton. Our John Burbidge was the eighth and youngest, born in 1900 in The Old Turnpike House at Cuckold's Green.

In 1904 disaster struck the family when farther – Frank Burbidge – died in his late 40s leaving a destitute widow still with her four youngest children to bring up. On the 3rd September 1904 mother, Mary, asked the vicar to help her place two of her children in the Muller Children's Home in Bristol*. Eleanor Burbidge (No. 6) stayed in the orphanage until she was placed in service on her 17th birthday. But little John had to wait another two years to follow his sister into the Home. This was because they wouldn't take sick children. John bore extensive scars on both legs as a result of being scalded in the groin at age four, about the time his father died. While the children were in the Home, mother moved into service in London.

John spoke well of his treatment there and didn't want to leave. But the custom was to place boys into an apprenticeship on their 14th birthday. He was put on a train to London but his mother sent him straight back to Bristol to join the army.

John Burbidge at War

On the outbreak of war John volunteered for operational service, and in November (still only 14 years old) he arrived in Zeebrugge to join the Wiltshire Regiment. The Wiltshires raised 10 Battalions, gained 60 Battle Honours and 1 Victoria Cross, and lost 5,200 men during the course of the war. Private Burbidge was in the 2nd Battalion, brought home from Gibraltar to become part of the 21st brigade in the 7th Division.

Whilst in the Battalion he fought in the First Battle of Ypres where they lost 7 officers and 76 men killed, 229 wounded and 18 Officers and 450 men captured. In 1915 they took part in a major assault at Neuve-Chapelle where again they suffered terribly by taking another 400 casualties. This was followed by many months of trench warfare before the Battle of Loos (another 400 casualties). The following year they transferred to the 30th Division for the Battles of Albert and the Transloy Ridges, at one point being called upon to bayonet their way through the enemy defenders (240 casualties in this action). In 1917 they took part in the pursuit of the German retreat to the Hindenburg line (losing 16 officers and 363 other ranks), the First and Second Battles of the Scarpe and the Battle of Pilkem Ridge, all at Ypres.

Alas! after all that, Private Burbidge's luck ran out. During the infamous Battle of Pozières the 2nd Wiltshires were in action near Royle in which they were outflanked, completely surrounded, and lost 22 officers and 600 other ranks. Burbidge was posted as missing, later reported to be wounded and later still reported killed in action on that day. He was 18 years old.

Commemoration

After the War he was posthumously awarded the 1914 Star, the Victory Medal and the British War Medal. Private Burbidge has no known grave but is commemorated on the Pozières Memorial.

And After?

While a branch of the Burbidge family lived for a time in two cottages in Back Lane it seems most likely that after the Great War the remaining Burbidges of this branch of the family had migrated away from Worton.

* *The Orphanage, on Ashley Down in Bristol, opened in 1845 and looked after about 2000 children. It was created by George Müller, a German minister, and was said to have been his atonement for his dissolute youth.*

Herbert Alfred Dunford

Herbert Alfred Dunford was brought up in Sideways Cottage, 51 High Street in Worton where he lived with his parents, his sister and three brothers. His father was a cowman born in Potterne, and mother came from Bulkington. In his teens Herbert became a general farm labourer.

Herbert Alfred Dunford at War

Private Herbert Dunford volunteered for the Army and joined the Welch Regiment in Cardiff. The Regiment raised 36 Battalions and was awarded 71 Battle Honours and 3 Victoria Crosses, losing 8,360 men during the course of the war.

He was 21 when he arrived in France on the 18th May 1915

whereupon he was sent to his regiment's 2nd Battalion which was part of the 3rd Brigade in the 1st Division. Having mobilised for war in early August 1914, the battalion went from its base at Bordon in Hampshire to land at Le Havre, there to begin operations on the Western Front. By the time Private Dunford joined, the battalion had already fought in the Battle of Mons and the subsequent retreat, the Battle of the Marne, the Battle of the Aisne, and the First Battle of Ypres, together with the winter operations of 1914-15.

Dunford was to serve in France for less than four months but nevertheless he saw action in the Battle of Aubers and the Battle of Loos, north of Vimy and Arras in Flanders.

The British strength on the Western Front had slowly grown, although precious troops, equipment and munitions were being consumed in the Gallipoli theatre and elsewhere. Compared with our small-scale efforts in the spring of 1915, the September attack at Loos by six divisions was a mighty offensive indeed - so much so that it was referred to at the time as 'The Big Push'. However, the British Army on the Western Front was not yet ready for a major offensive and was being committed by an Ally to a battle not of its choosing and on unsuitable ground.

The opening of the battle on the 25th September 1915 was noteworthy for the first use of poison gas by the British Army and, despite heavy casualties, there was considerable success on this first day in breaking into the deep enemy positions near Loos and Hulluch. On day two of the battle the advance of Dunford's 2nd Welch and others came under severe fire, including point-blank artillery, not to mention British shellfire falling among them in this murderous area too. By about 1.00pm only a thin line had reached the virtually undamaged German wire. All attempts to cut the wire failed with heavy casualties, and the remaining men took cover in the long grass. At a shouted order to retire, men withdrew - many being hit by machine-gun fire as they did so. Those who did not retire were killed or captured.

It was here that Private Dunford lost his life (along with 310 other men from his Battalion). He was reported missing presumed dead on that Sunday, the 26th September 1915, and he has no known grave.

Private Dunford was awarded the 1914-15 Star Campaign Medal of the British Empire, the British War Medal and the Victory Medal. All were awarded posthumously and would have been sent to the family after the war.

Commemoration

As well as being commemorated on the brass plaque in Christ Church, Private Dunford's name is also inscribed on the Loos Memorial.

And After?

Herbert's mother, Mary Jane Dunford, having lost two of her children, lived 'til she was 85 and died in 1948. Her eldest child, Elsie, married William Phillips and lived in Sandleaze Cottage; they had no children. Herbert's older brother, Arthur James Dunford, married in 1907 and they had five children born before and during the war. Their fourth, Stanley Arthur, married Dorothy Bowden in 1935, and one of this couple's children, Grenville Dunford, lives in Devizes today. Arthur James is buried in the Christ Church churchyard with his wife Beatrice.

Herbert Owen Few

This branch of the Few family were farmers who came to Worton from Urchfont in the early 19th Century. Stephen Few and his wife Eliza (Staples) had seven children of whom Herbert Owen was number three. The family had evidently prospered as farmers, having moved from a 91 acre farm with two employees in Urchfont to 172 acres at Manor Farm here in Worton. At the start of the Great War the children ranged in age from 15 to 26 and their uncle, also a farmer, lived with them too.

From 1914 there was a pressing need to feed the nation and as father and uncle were both well over 60, two sons remained at home to keep the farm going, releasing the other two to go off to Kitchener's army. Nevertheless, in 1916 the 26 year old Herbert Few applied to the Military Exemption Tribunal to remain at home too, claiming his father and brother were unfit to work. The tribunal concluded 'Mischief' so off he went to enrol in the Durham Light Infantry.

Herbert Owen Few at War

The Durham Light Infantry was awarded 67 Battle Honours, six Victoria Crosses and lost 12,530 men during the course of the war, by the end of which the regiment had raised 42 various battalions, together with regimental labour units, into which were drafted men medically graded as unfit for service in the front line. In 1917 these labour units had grown into a national Labour Corps containing 389,900 men, and it was to the 3rd Company of this Corps that Private Herbert Few was transferred.

Labour Corps units were often deployed for work within range of the enemy's guns, and in the crises of March and April 1918 on the Western Front Labour Corps units were used as emergency infantry. Nevertheless, few records remain of the daily activities and locations of Corps units. We do know however that Private Few was injured in the war and repatriated for treatment in the Special Military Surgical Hospital at Headington in Oxford (which over the years grew into the Nuffield Orthopaedic Hospital).

One account has it that he died in the military hospital on the 11th August 1919 and that his body was then returned to his parents. Another says he returned home earlier to be nursed by the family until he died of his wounds. In any event he was buried in the Christ Church churchyard aged thirty (Row 19 Plot 11). Private Few was posthumously awarded the Victory Medal and the British War Medal.

Commemoration

Herbert Owen Few is commemorated on the memorial plaque on the north wall inside the church.

And After?

When Herbert died in 1919 his father Stephen Few was 72 and no doubt thinking of easing up on the running of Manor Farm. Two of Herbert's brothers, both of whom remained bachelors, continued to work the farm into the mid 1960s. They are buried together in the Christ Church churchyard. Another brother, Lionel, farmed Watt's Farm, now known as Willowbrook Farm on the High Street. He had also joined up for the Great War and served as a driver in the Royal Field Artillery. He died in 1974 and is buried with our Herbert Owen

Few (the two soldiers together) in the churchyard.

The Goss's - the well known Worton farming family - are descended from Herbert Owen's elder sister Dorothy Few.

A story passed down in the village has it that the Holly bush behind Herbert's grave in the churchyard sprang from the berries carried on a Christmas spray placed there each year by the Few family. This spray they brought from the tree in their garden at Manor Farm, which also, we understand, used to provide many villagers with their Christmas Holly.

The Fielding Brothers

The Fielding's have lived and worked here from before the Glorious Revolution (1689). By the end of the 19th century, one Thomas Fielding had risen from cowman to become a market gardener living on ***Mount Pleasant*** here in Worton. They had eleven children all told, of whom William Henry was number five and Arthur John number seven. They both attended the village school and helped in the market garden until enlisting in the army.

The Fielding Sons at War

William Henry Fielding became a member of the army gym staff at Le Marchant barracks and in 1910 at the age of 17 enlisted in the Dorsetshire regiment. In 1912 he was sent with the 2nd Battalion to India. For the Great War the Dorsetshire Regiment raised 12 battalions and received 57 battle honours, losing 1,060 men during its course.

At the outbreak of war the 20 year old William henry was stationed with his battalion in Poona as part of the 16th Brigade in the Poona Division. They deployed to the Persian Gulf in November 1914.

The situation in 1916 had the Turks pursuing the retreating 6th Poona division to Kut and soon surrounded and cut them off. British forces in Mesopotamia were ordered to advance along the river Tigris to relieve Kut, but they ran into strong opposition and themselves received some hard knocks. Although they got close to Kut the garrison there was surrendered to the Turks on the 29th April

1916; a massive blow to the British Army comparable to the surrender in Singapore in the Second World War.

Conditions in Mesopotamia defy description; 120 F was common and there was appalling sickness and death from disease. Units fell short of men and reinforcements were half-trained and ill-equipped, leading to very high casualty rates. On the 29th April 1916 over 12,000 British and Empire troops surrendered and were then marched north to Turkey with little food and water but much brutality. Among the 12,000 there were 350 man of the 2nd Dorset's captured at Kut and Amara. Only 70 survived their captivity.

Private William Fielding, one of the captives, died of chronic enteritis on the 20th October 1916 while a prisoner of war in Andana Turkey. He was 23 years old and was posthumously awarded the Victory Medal, the British War Medal and in 1915 star.

Commemoration

William Fielding is buried in the Baghdad (North Gate) Cemetery, located in what is now a very sensitive area of the Al-Russafa District of Baghdad. At the moment it is not possible for the commonwealth War Grave Commission to maintain its cemeteries and memorials in Iraq. For the time being a two volume Roll of honour listing all casualties is available for viewing at the commissions Head office in Maidenhead.

Arthur John Fielding joined the colours in late 1914 at the age of 17. When he enlisted at Devizes he became first, like his brother before him, a member of the Wiltshire Special Reserve. He volunteered for service overseas and was sent to join the 5th battalion of the Duke of Edinburgh's (Wiltshire Regiment) at Lala Bada, Gallipoli in November 1915. This battalion had already seen fierce fighting at Gallipoli and had just been overrun by a Turkish Division led by Mustapha Kemal, with half of them never being seen again. The main enemy then became dysentery and jaundice.

They were evacuated to Egypt in January 1916 and, after a rest in Port Said, were reinforced with 750 new men. The next month the battalion moved to Mesopotamia and in April 1916 were part of the force which attempted to relieve the garrison at Kut al Amara (which included his brother William. The 5th Wiltshire's attacked Turkish trenches, first at Hannah, then at Sanna-I-Yat but all efforts to relieve the garrison failed.

Private Arthur Fielding, then just 18 years old, dies of wounds in that battle on 18th June 1916 in a military hospital in Amara. Like his brother William he was posthumously awarded the victory medal. The British War Medal and the 1915 star.

Commemoration

Arthur Fielding is buried in the Amara War Cemetery, but due to its location in a sensitive part of modern day Iraq arrangements fir his commemoration are the same as those for his brother set out above.

And After?

The Fielding brothers parents retired to Potterne but father died just before war broke out. Mother was then to suffer the loss of two of her boys and she herself died soon after it was all over. Other brothers Frederick Fielding, farmed at Cherry Orchard on the road south from Worton where successive generations right down to the present day have continued to farm.

Henry Francis Harris

Henry Francis Harris was the eldest of five children of the Worton Shoemaker who plied his trade here in the last quarter of the 19th Century. His name was Thomas Harris and he lived and worked in the house between the Rose and Crown and Oak Cottage on the north side of the High Street. Henry was born in 1876.

In the 1890s henry Francis Harris was a farm labourer before he moved out of the family home in Worton to board in the High street in Avebury, next door to the Post Office there. This is where he learned his craft as a blacksmith. He settled in Avebury, in 1911 married Sarah Jane Farley, and set up home with her in Bray Street in Avebury.

Henry Francis Harris at War

Unfortunately, we know very little of henry's war service because his papers were lost when the Army Records office was fire bombed in WWII. We do know that he took his trade into the Army because he joined the Royal Army Veterinary Corps as a ***Shoeing Smith Corporal.***

Corporal Harris served in the Middle East during the Great War and ended up working in the 26th Veterinary Hospital located in Alexandria Egypt. Although he survived combat operations he was hospitalized at the end of the Great War and died there on 14th January 1919 at the age of 43. He was posthumously awarded the Victory Medal and the British War Medal.

Commemoration

Corporal Henry Francis Harris is buried in the Hadra War Memorial Cemetery in Alexandria Egypt (Grave H.92).

And After?

Henry's younger brother, William John Harris who was born in 1878 became a cattleman while still living in the family home. He stayed in Worton, died in 1943 at the age of 65, and was buried in the Christ Church Churchyard on the 26th November 1943. There were three younger sisters one of whom lived with the Burbidge family on back lane close to the then vicarage.

David Waite (Relative of villager Roger Wiltshire)

Reserved occupations were sometimes overlooked, but these were vital roles which some men and women played during the Great War. While many young men willingly volunteered to fight or were conscripted, there were key jobs which still had to be done by those who had to stay behind.

David was a shepherd in Wiltshire, part of the vital effort to keep the nation and troops fed. In particular in the latter stages of the war, where Germany attempted to blockade and starve Britain into submission.

David Waite. Reserved occupation

RELATIVES OF CURRENT VILLAGERS REMEMBERED

Relatives of David Johnson

William Holland (David's grandfather on his mother's side of the family) 1889-1936. Survived the war. He was the son of a Lancashire coal miner (from several generations of coal miners). William Holland was a coal face worker, one of the most dangerous jobs.

During WW1 he was involved in digging tunnels under German trenches. He survived the war and returned to see his daughter Ethel Holland (David Johnson's mother) born in late 1918. On return from the war he went back down the mines until his death in 1936.Photos: Photos of William Holland in 1917.

Ernest Johnson (David's grandfather on his father's side of the family) 1890 – 1969. Survived the war.

Johnson brothers Ernest, William and Harry were all involved in WW1 in different ways. They came from a family line of Royal Navy members and Royal Navy dock yard workers in Chatham and Sheerness dockyards on the Isle of Sheppey in Kent. (David's great grandfather William, was a master rigger in the dockyard, where HMS Victory was built. His Gt, Gt Grandfather Henry (2) and His Gt, Gt, Gt Grandfather Henry (1) were both RN Master shipwrights).

The three brothers (Ernest, William and Harry) had different roles in WW1. Ernest was a boiler maker and was involved in building warships. Harry was a Royal Navy OD Seaman and served on board and William was a ships rigger. All three survived the war. Ernest and his wife had Alan (David's father) in 1924.

Other family members, the Osborne's, were in the Army, but no detailed family records currently exist for them except some of the photos below.

Photo of the three Johnson brothers together. Photos of Osborne family members during WW1.

Relatives of Christine Johnson

Hill Brothers

Percy Hill was born in 1891 in Portsea where his family owned their own bakery.

Percy joined the regular army The Kings Liverpool Regiment 1st Batt and was sent to The Northwest frontier with his brother Sidney. On their return Percy remained in the army and was sent to fight in France. He died on August 23 1914 at Mons.

He is remembered with honour

La Ferte-Sous-Jouarre Memorial, Seine –et-Marne France.

Archibald Hill was born in 1889 in Portsea. His family owned their own bakery.
His brothers had all joined the forces and Archie followed. He joined the Navy and survived the war.
On his return he met his wife and moved to South Africa and finally to Australia.

Harold Hill was born in Portsea 1892. His family owned their bakery where he worked until he was able to leave home. Where upon he joined the Merchant Navy and sailed to Australia.

He married his wife Myrtle and they had two children. When news of his brother's death reach him he took it very badly. He immediately joined the navy where he was a chef and set sail for England. He never returned to Australia but he survived the war. Many of the crew on the ship he served were Australian and were about to embark home when the killer flu hit them. Most died in Liverpool where he is buried. (16,000,000 died worldwide). How sad!!

Sidney Hill was born in 1886 while his family was travelling in Swansea. The family moved to Portsea where they settled opening their own bakery.

Sidney was an apprentice baker but decided to join the regular army for several years. On his discharge he returned to worked in the family bakery until his brother Percy was killed at Mons on the 23 August in 1914and he re-joined the army.

Sidney was also posted to the front but was injured from gassing. He returned home and married Isabella in 1922 and they lived in Poplar the East End of London.

Sidney had 6 children but was plagued by ill health all his life due to the gassing. He managed work on the docks when he was well but took a turn for the worst and died Christmas Eve 1935. Leaving his family with little finances. Although very poor all his children worked hard and made a success of their life. Sidney Hill. Kings Rifles. Died from the long term effects of mustard gas in 1935 at age of 49.

Ernest Spokes

Ernest Spokes was born 1898 in Reading Berkshire. His father was a brick maker. He was the oldest child in his family and was an intelligent child who passed a scholarship to the Bluecoat School.

His father and sister died in 1903 of TB, a year after his brother was born.

He joined the 1st Bn Royal Berkshire Regiment in 1915 when he was 17. He was what is referred to as a boy soldier and should not have been sent to war. He was assigned to the Western front at the age of 17 and then was quickly reassigned to Mesopotamia. This was a terrible war and many died.

Ernest survived the war but never returned home afterwards. He died of yellow fever and dysentery on July 30th July 1921 age 23 years.

Ernest is buried in Baghdad (North Gate) war cemetery Iraq.

His brother (my father) never spoke of him but every year my father made us remember all those that died during that period where his face showed an immense sadness, especially as the war was just finishing when he was still 15 and he couldn't join up and follow his older brother.

Private E.G.Spokes 1st Battalion Royal Berkshire Regiment died age 23 30th July 1021 in Iraq.

Relative of Giles Collins

Great Uncle Giles

Giles Robert Daubeney was born on 13th September 1895 and died, aged 19, on 23rd April 1915.

He was one of four children born to Mrs Lilian Daubeney and the Reverend Arthur Giles Daubeney, vicar of Herne in Kent:

Margaret Helen (my grandmother) (1893 – 1958), Cecily Marian (1894 – 1985), Giles Robert (1895 – 1915), Ralph Thomas (1897 – 1926).

Giles was educated at Bradfield College and was an undergraduate at Selwyn College, Cambridge in 1913. He was commissioned as a 2nd Lieutenant in the Royal West Kent Regiment and was posted to the British Expeditionary Force on 25th January 1915. He took part in the 2nd Battle of Ypres and, when in action at St Julien on 23rd April 1915, he was shot whilst crawling back for cover after attending a wounded man.

He is commemorated on a private brass memorial tablet in Ampney St Peter's church Gloucestershire and also on the Menin Gate Memorial (panel 45/47), Ypres, Belgium.

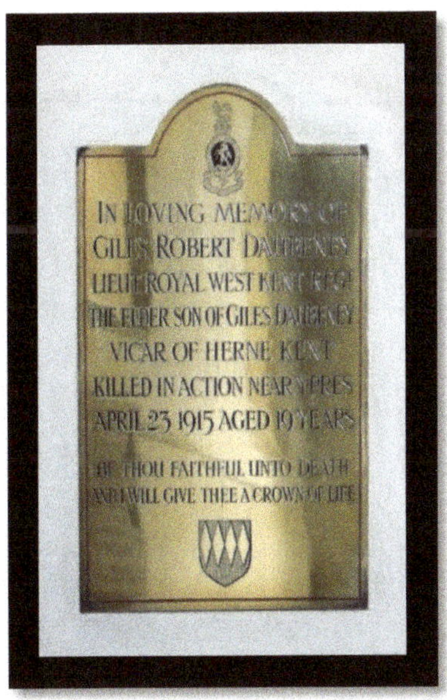

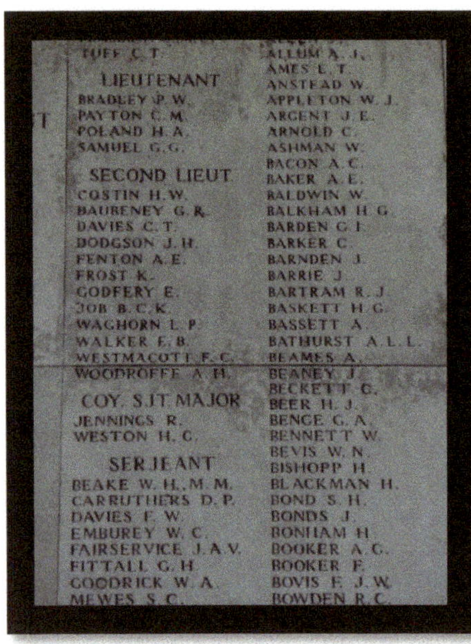

He is also commemorated at St Bartholomew's Church, Herne Bay: 'As the visitor passes through, he or she will see to their right the wooden framed chapel, known as the Memorial or All Souls' Chapel which was designed by Caroe and erected by the family of Captain Henry Hogarth Bell (stepson of the Reverend Giles Daubeney) as a memorial to him and Lieutenant Giles Robert Daubeney, the Vicar's own son, both killed in action in the Great War. The paneling of this chapel was placed in memory of Ralph Thomas Daubeney of the RAP Reserve, who died in South Africa in 1926. The names of all these were carved and painted in gold against the paneling, and the chapel contains family heraldry. It is used today as a place of prayer'.

My grandmother was just 22 when her brother, Giles, died. She loved him dearly and spoke about him frequently throughout her life (she outlived him by 43 years). My aunt Cicely, Giles' other sister, came to live with us in her old age. Although she could not remember very much on a day-to-day basis, she regularly talked about her brother, over 60 years after his death. He must have been a remarkable boy. Who knows what sort of man he might have become had he not given his life on 23rd April 1915?

Relatives of Paul Sperring

World War 1

Lot (Percy) Sperring – Grandfather of Paul and Nigel Sperring – Born 1900 Weston-Super-Mare

Joined the Somerset Light Infantry in 1916 and was sent to Mesoptamia (modern day Iraq). He served alongside 41st Indian Brigade defending lines of communication. He was then attached to 56th Indian Brigade and finished the war attached to 14th Indian Division and ended the war at Tekrit north of Baghdad

Frederick George Osborn - Grandfather of Paul and Nigel Sperring – Born 1900 Coulsdon Surrey

Joined the Merchant Navy on 10 July 1916 and served as a "Trimmer" on two ships in WW1, 'SS Balmoral Castle' and 'SS Vauban' Between 1916 and 1918 the ships transported American Troops. In 1919 'SS Balmoral Castle' repatriated Australian troops

'Trimmers' used shovels and wheelbarrows to move coal around the bunkers in order to keep the coal level, and to shovel the coal down the coal chute to the firemen below, who shovelled it into the furnaces. If too much coal built up on one side of a coal bunker, the **ship** would actually list to that side.

Relatives of Robin and Judy Shercliff

One Family Two Grandfathers

As with many folk looking back to the Great War one family's research has thrown up two grandfathers from opposite sides of the world who fought together for pretty much the whole war.

Frank Shercliff	George Claxton Banyard
With an Army Number of *168*, the 26 year old Frank Shercliff, a mining engineer from Bright, Victoria Australia travelled to Melbourne in early August 1914 to become one of the very first to enlist in the Australian Imperial Force. His subsequent career in the Great War took him first to Cairo on the 4th December. (Although destined for training in England, Salisbury Plain was full to the brim with the Canadian Army; conditions on the Plain being so bad that no more could be fitted in.) In Egypt their training for France was interrupted in 1915 when, on the 24th April, they sailed to Turkey and Shercliff went ashore at Gallipoli on ANZAC Day, the 25th. Details of the Gallipoli campaign are well known; Shercliff's work consisted largely of fighting and construction works underground, frequently in sound of the enemy just a few yards away. That was when the Australian soldiers were first christened *Diggers*. As with very many of the troops in Gallipoli Shercliff contracted enteric typhoid fever and was hospitalised in Alexandria and Cairo. In March 1916 he was well enough to be sent by train and steamer through the submarine infested Mediterranean to Toulon France and thence by train straight to The Somme, arriving in June 1916. The Australian charnel house battles in which he fought at Pozières, Fromelles, Mouquet Farm, Ypres, the assault on the Siegfried/Hindenberg Line, Arras, Vimy, Billecourt Ridge, Messines and Paschendaele are all well known. After nearly four years in the front lines, many months of them fighting underground, Shercliff was hospitalised back to Melbourne in August 1918.	Mrs Judy Shercliff's 25 year old accountant grandfather George Banyard travelled to Norwich to enlist in the Norfolk Regiment (The Holy Boys) on practically the same day - 4th August 1914 - as Frank Shercliff did in Melbourne. His career in the Great War followed an uncannily similar path in that his brigade (the East Anglian) became part of the 54th Infantry Division destined for the Dardanelles, there to bivouac on the beach in Suvla Bay on the 10th August 1915. After very severe fighting in the ANZAC Sector against the Turks alongside Shercliff's Division, and with his battalion reduced through casualties to one fifth of its original strength, Banyard's Regiment was evacuated to Egypt. Here the two grandfathers diverged in that Banyard spent 1916 defending the Suez Canal against attack and then in February 1917 marched across the Sinai Desert towards Gaza and the Palestine front. More fierce fighting led to the fall of Gaza (in which Banyard's battalion sustained 657 Casualties, many through hand to hand fighting). They continued with Allenby's advance and took part in the capture of Jerusalem on the 9th December 1917. Thereafter, Banyard's path converged with that of Shercliff and the Australians in that, having transferred to a different battalion in the Norfolk Regiment he moved to the Western Front in France mainly raiding the German lines when the opportunity arose, principally in the Messines, Arras and Cambrai battles. Shortly before the Armistice in November 1918 Banyard was caught by a gas attack, from the effects of which he suffered for the rest of his life.
And After	
Soon after returning to Australia the Spanish Flu epidemic devastated Melbourne. Frank Shercliff took his family to Perak in the Federated Malay States to manage the tin mines when, in 1941, in a hastily formed Dad's Army and at the age of 53, he fought against the Japanese invasion down through Malaya to end up in Changi PoW Camp. He did however spend time outside the gaol after being invited to help build the Burma Railway. He died aged 66.	After the Great War, George Banyard resumed his accountancy profession even though being severely incapacitated from his gas attack which nevertheless did not prevent him making a full contribution to the USAAC bombing effort in the Second World War. He died aged 68.

Relative of Margaret Tucker

In Memory of

Private W STROUD

5th Bn., Wiltshire Regiment
who died aged 19 on Thursday, 25th January 1917.

Private STROUD was the son of William and Sophia G. Stroud, of Axford, Marlborough.

Remembered with honour
AMARA WAR CEMETERY, Iraq.

Relative of Cheryl Hailstone

In Memory of
Private ALFRED AGG

15370, 2nd Bn., Gloucestershire Regiment
who died
on 07 March 1915
Private AGG

Remembered with honour
YPRES (MENIN GATE) MEMORIAL

Commemorated in perpetuity by
the Commonwealth War Graves Commission

In Memory of
Serjeant JOHN AGG

20435, 1st Coy., Machine Gun Corps (Inf)
who died age 29
on 14 July 1916
Serjeant AGG, Brother of Mrs. E. Little, of The Bungalow, Kempsford Fairford, Glos.

Remembered with honour
THIEPVAL MEMORIAL

Commemorated in perpetuity by
the Commonwealth War Graves Commission

Relative of Bryn Evans

The family featured here was centred upon a very small farming village.

Barkby in Leicestershire – population at the time, probably about 200.

My Grandfather Gerry Underwood Senior and his son (my uncle) Gerry Underwood Junior.

Nothing very unusual in the photos until we look at their experiences.

Gerry senior received shrapnel wounds to his back at Ypres during WW1.

Gerry junior received shrapnel wounds to his back at Ypres during the early days of WW2.

He was later evacuated from Dunkirk beach and then survived a bomb attack on his hospital ship.

Sadly, I know nothing more because as a youngster, I failed to question either of them for more details. As in so many cases, it is now too late! They didn't talk and we didn't question. My knowledge is simply what I overheard in family conversations.

I hope that this important exhibition will serve as a reminder to everyone, young and not so young, to question the older generation. It could be very interesting. It often is.
Family history, village history, national history is our heritage.

I am sad to say, I know very little about WW1. It was too recent to be taught in my history lessons and probably, too painful for family discussion.

However, because I was born a few years before the start of WW2, I have some very vivid memories. The photo of Gerry Senior with his pig I remember very well. The year I guess, was about 1942. It was taken in his back garden.

During the second world war the government allowed people to keep pigs in their gardens to help with food production. Friends and neighbours would collect food waste (called swill) to feed the pig. I recall Grandad boasting that his pig would be 20 score. This was a reference to the pig's weight. In our pre-decimal world a dozen was twelve and a score was 20. Therefore 20 score translates as 20 x 20 = 400 lbs. A huge pig by today's standard.

The pig was then slaughtered and shared by the whole family. My grandparents had 6 children. My parents had 6 children. I had a lot of cousins. I don't remember having a lot of pork! Mind you, nothing was wasted. Everything was eaten from its feet (trotters) to its innards (chitterlings) to its head which was made into brawn.

Bryn Evans, Worton

Relatives of Rob and Val Dodd

Albert Wiltshire June 1895- April 1987

I first met Albert Wiltshire Senior when I met his granddaughter Valerie in 1970. When asking Winnie, his partner to get a cup of tea, he used Urdu words after he asked for tea, which he told me meant "Hurry up". He had picked up some Hirdu when fighting with the Indian Army in the Great War. So I asked him where he had served! Which was in Mesopotamia or as Albert said "it is called Iraq now".

This photo of him on horseback was taken in Baghdad where he was in the Royal Artillery. A lot of men who fought there died of disease and fever within weeks of getting there. Albert caught the fever and survived, he reckons he survived because he never passed out. One evening a Medical Officer came in to the ward to see him, he asked the Orderly how was he getting on, and the Orderly said "He is still hanging in Sir". The Doctor looked over at Albert, and Albert described him to me, jet black hair with a parting down the centre, monocle and a David Niven type moustache. He looked into Albert's eyes, and said to the Orderly "This man has a black heart" Albert recovered and said he had never had a days illness since.

His mates had saved up their rum ration and some food, as they weren't on duty the next day decided to have a Beano, all the food was thrown into a pot and cooked, and they drunk their rum mixed with a little water. Albert wondered into the desert to relieve himself, tripped, fell on what he thought was a wicker basket, by the sound it made, and because of drink fell straight off to sleep, when he awoke, he found it was a dead camel that broke his fall. When I asked him about the Turks that he had fought, he said "Johnny Turk was alright" by this he meant they were aggressive soldiers.

He also said when he come out of the army after the war, he couldn't settle down so had a trip to India. Thereafter he returned to Hemel Hempstead, married and had six sons, two are still living, Frank living in Milborne Port, Dorset, and Jack in Hemel Hempstead, Hertfordshire.

Relative of Mark Fisher

Lost in the Desert

My grandfather on my mother's side, William Hardy, served in the British Army in Palestine at the end of the Great War. In charge of a supply chain of mules, he got lost in the desert until some friendly tribesmen showed him the way to the camp.

That was the only experience he would ever talk about during that conflict.

This picture shows him in uniform on horseback. After the War he went back to his job as a bench fitter, at the Dennis works in Guildford, where my mother was born, raised and eventually married.

Mark Fisher

Relative of John Lane

JOHN HENRY LANE (1892-1916)

John Henry was the oldest of six children, born to George Robert Lane and Maria Ryding in Horwich, near Bolton, Lancashire, on April 10th 1892.

John's grandparents, Samuel and Emily Lane, had travelled with his very young father, George Robert, from Sixpenny Handley in Dorset in the early 1870's, passing through Little Langford, Wiltshire, to Crewe and subsequently to Horwich in Lancashire, where opportunities for employment in the expanding railway industry presented themselves. For many generations up to that point the Lane family had been agricultural labourers around Sixpenny Handley, Dorset, traceable back to the early 1700's.

On the outbreak of war in 1914, aged 22, he enlisted with the 10th (Service) Battalion of the Royal Welsh Fusiliers. This was formed at Wrexham as part of the Kitchener's Third Army (K3). They travelled to training camp at Codford, Salisbury Plain, to join the 76th Brigade, 25th Division, and then billeted in Bournemouth overwinter in 1914/15.

In April 1915 they moved to Romsey and via Winchester, Alresford (26th May), Odiham (29th May), to Barrosa Barracks, Aldershot, 3rd June 1915 for final training.

On 27th September 1915 they mobilised for war, and 27 officers along with 822 rank and file under the command of colonel WRH

Beresford-Ash railed to Folkestone in two special trains, embarked on the SS Victoria, disembarked at Boulogne at 10.30pm, and marched to rest camp.

On the 15th of October 1915 they transferred with 76th Brigade to 3rd Division and engaged in various actions on the Western Front, including the Battle of The Ancre.

The Battle of the Ancre 13–18 November, was the final large scale British attack of the Battle of the Somme in 1916, before the winter weather forced a pause in British attacks until the new year. The Battalion attacked the Serre trenches at 5.45am on a 250 yard front between Mark Copse and Matthew Copse.John Henry Lane was killed on the first day of this Battle, one of hundreds listed as missing on the War Record for that day. He is commemorated on the Thiepval memorial (pier and face 4A), one of 923 members of the Royal welsh fusiliers, a small proportion of over 72 thousand allied soldiers who died during the Battle of the Somme, and who have no known grave.

Relative of Alison Garside

Lockhart Samuel MacVean (Lockie) – 1916-1985

My father lived in the countryside just outside Leeds. As he was the eldest of four children he quite often spent holidays with his Uncle and Aunt Bryson in Glasgow. His Uncle was in shipping so when Dad reached 16 and the war was still raging, Uncle suggested that he apply to Marconi Ltd. to train as a Wireless Telegraphy Operator at their depot in Newcastle. With the war the need for wireless operators increased dramatically as increasing numbers of ships found it essential to be fitted with wireless, operated by at least two operators for 24 hours cover. Available operators were drafted into the Navy, leaving the Merchant Navy with a significant shortfall and prompting a major recruitment campaign.

Dad in dress uniform.

Two months later the Fontinca was torpedoed and the SS War Roman came to the rescue. Sadly, when a further attempt was made to resume the voyage, the War Roman ran aground the men being rescued once again by the SS War Norman. Two days later, she too met with disaster; this time aid was given by the light cruiser HMS Topaze which carried out salvage work.

Dad and his fellow telegraph operator, Mr MacPherson, who were employed directly by Marconi rather than the shipping firm, were subsequently transferred to the SS Borderer as passengers, making the remaining voyage home via Oran, where they coaled and Oporto, Portugal, where the Borderer unloaded her cargo of rice. Two postcards to his brother say that he hoped to be home in a month.

After a period of leave (2 weeks) Dad, now known as the 'Jonah' was finally demobbed on November 17th 1919.

p.s. he never did learn to swim!

It is strange to think that in a few years his youngest brother Donald, having survived Dunkirk, spent the rest of the second war in Cairo in the Military Police, their mother once again looking anxiously for letters from a son in Africa.

This is an account of his final voyage on the SS (screw steamer) Joseph Davis, with details from his diary which was written largely on postcards:

After leaving Glasgow they first docked at Pauillac on the Gironde Estuary north of Bordeaux where they unloaded coal (which must have been needed in large quantities for fuelling the ships). Then on to Bilbao on Spain's north coast, followed by Douro, Portugal.

On the way to Genoa the ship stopped briefly at the small town of Aguilas to load at sea (due to the rocky shore) by means of lighters.

After Genoa the ship sailed on to Port Said and the entrance to the Suez Canal and the Red Sea. Here they met with disaster. The Red Sea was a dangerous area: the eastern bank was held by the Ottoman Turks and there were hostilities between them and the British whose aim was to protect the important trade route through the Suez Canal. As the Joseph Davis approached Aden, then an important coaling and watering station,she was wrecked off the coast of Somaliland. The crew were picked up by the SS Fontinca and remained with her whilst salvage was arranged.

Relative of Andrew Stock

19th November 1918

SECOND LIEUTENANT CHARLES PERCY TOMKINS, Middlesex Regiment, was wounded severely in the thigh on August 24 and during treatment for his wound in a London hospital died on October 29 from double pneumonia following an attack of influenza. He was educated at Merchant Taylors school, after which he went to Brazil, where he spent some years in business. He took a great interest in athletics for which he held many medals and prizes and was an excellent shot. In July 1914, he came over on a visit to England and enlisted in the ranks three or four weeks after the outbreak of war. After serving 10 months in France and Flanders, he was 14 months in Salonika, and while there was awarded a good conduct stripe. After about two years active service he was granted leave and was recommended for a commission. On completing a course in an officer cadet battalion at St John's College, Cambridge, he obtained his commission and was gazetted to the Middlesex regiment, in which he had served as a private. The following is an extract from a letter to his family written by one of his men who brought him in from No Man's Land after he had been wounded :-"We all hope he will not come out here again, although we should very much like to be under his command, for he gave us courage through a hail of machine-gun bullets and issued his orders to his men as if on a parade ground in England."

2nd Lt Charles Percy Tomkins
6th Middlesex Regiment
Enlisted Private 31.8.14
Wounded near Ervillers 24.8.18
Died in hospital (London) 20.10.18

Relatives of Rachel Ganuszko

Alfred George Haberland

Great Grandfather, born 4th October 1895 in Bethnal Green East.

During WW1, went into a special regiment for sons of German immigrants:

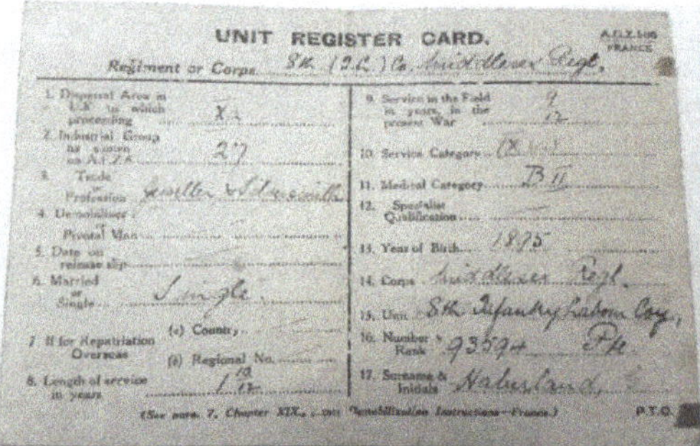

UNIT REGISTER CARD.

Regiment or Corps 8th (?) Co. Middlesex Regt.

1. Dispersal Area in U.K. to which proceeding X
2. Industrial Group for A.F.Z.8 27
3. Trade or Profession Jeweller & Silversmith
4. Demobiliser or Pivotal Man
5. Date on release slip
6. Married or Single Single
7. If for Repatriation Overseas (a) Country (b) Regional No.
8. Length of service in years 1 10/12
9. Service in the Field in years in the present War 9/12
10. Service Category
11. Medical Category B II
12. Specialist Qualification
13. Year of Birth 1895
14. Corps Middlesex Regt.
15. Unit 8th Infantry Labour Coy.
16. Number & Rank 93594 Pte
17. Surname & Initials Haberland

(See para. 7, Chapter XIX., Demobilization Instructions—France.)

P.T.O.

(Alfred is standing up in the photo)

Alfred went to France in 1917 as part of the Middlesex Regiment to "clear up".

Cap badge of the Middlesex Regiment

Frederick Knight

Great-grandfather (paternal grandmother's father).

Born 9th April 1896. Worked for the Ministry of Labour including during WW1.

Edward James McLaren

Father of Frederick Knight's wife Milicent.

Born in 1875 in St Quivox, Ayrshire.

Was a musician in the Royal Marines eventually becoming a conductor in the Royal Marines

William "Bob" Thomas Carlyon 

Great-grandfather (maternal grandfather's father).

Born in Liskeard, Cornwall. Became a post boy upon leaving school before becoming a postman.

At the outbreak of WW1, he joined the Duke of Cornwall's Light Infantry as a machine gunner. He saw service in the Middle east and India.

Bob survived the war and joined the Police in 1922 (he remained in the police during WW2).

Army Form Z. 21.

CERTIFICATE of* ~~Discharge~~ / ~~Transfer to Reserve~~ / Disembodiment / ~~Demobilization~~ on Demobilization.

Regtl. No. 94598 Rank Private

Names in full Carlyon William Thomas (Surname first)

Unit and Regiment or Corps from which *~~Discharged~~ Disembodied ~~Transferred to Reserve~~ 256th Coy M.G.C.

Enlisted on the 12th November 1914

For 4th Batt D.C.L.I.

(Here state Regiment or Corps to which first appointed)

Also served in ...

Only Regiments or Corps in which the Soldier served since August 4th, 1914 are to be stated. If inapplicable, this space is to be ruled through in ink and initialed.

†Medals and Decorations awarded during present engagement: Nil / Auth Prior to 11-11-18

*Has / ~~Has not~~ served Overseas on Active Service.

Place of Rejoining in case of emergency: Fovant — Medical Category A1

Specialist Military qualifications: Nil — Year of birth 1894

He is* ~~Discharged~~ / ~~Transferred to Army Reserve~~ / Disembodied / ~~Demobilized~~ on 24th April 1919 in consequence of Demobilization.

Signature and Rank.

Officer i/c M.G.C. Records. 91 York St S.W.1 (Place).

* Strike out whichever is inapplicable. † The word "Nil" to be inserted when necessary.

(20996). Wt. W 8211—P.P. 2329. 3,000m. 1/19. D & S. (E 1256.)

WARNING.—If this Certificate is lost a duplicate cannot be issued. You should therefore on no account part with it or forward it by post when applying for a situation.

envelope to the Secretary, War Office, London, S.W.1.

British Army Service Records 1914-1920 Transcription

First name(s)	Alfred George
Last name	Haberland
Age	20
Birth year	1897
Birth county	Middlesex
Birth country	England
Service number	G/93594
Regiment	Middlesex Regiment
Unit / Battalion	30th Battalion
Year	1917
Series	WO 363
Series description	WO 363 - First World War service records 'burnt documents'
Archive	The National Archives
Record set	British Army Service Records
Category	Military, armed forces & conflict
Subcategory	First World War
Collections from	Great Britain

URL of this page: http://search.findmypast.co.uk/record?i
363-4%2f7405156%2f4%2f51

Alfred's army records

During WW2, Alfred served in the home guard in 1942.

Edward "Eddie" Haberland

As another of Frank's sons, Eddie served in the 1st Middlesex Regiment (D company 20208) during WW1 (the special regiment for sons of Germans).

After the war he worked as a projectionist in the Plaza Theatre, London.

Relatives of Dot Francis

Lily was my maternal grandmother and was born into a family of 10 children. Most of the children were born at Fulwood Barracks in Preston. On her father's discharge from the army the family moved to Liverpool.

In 1916 four of Lily's brothers joined the army.

Charles was born in 1890 and died in1916.

He was in the 1st Battalion' North Lancs Regiment. The regiment was involved in the defence of Ypres at Langemarck and the Battles of Neuve Chapelle, Aubers Ridge in 1915 and the Somme, Arras and Pachendale in 1917. Records show Charles was cared for at Wittingham Assylum. Many of the returning wounded soldiers that died are buried in the hospital grounds.

Albert Hunt 1891 and died 1916

He was a private in the Cheshire Regiment 15th Battalion. He was killed in action at the Battle of Somme. He is commemorated at the Thiepval Memoeial. Records show his mother Emma received a gratuity of £6 – 7shillings.

Stephen Hunt was in born 1893 and died 1916.

He was a member of the Kings Liverpool Regiment and died of his wounds in Flanders.

Five Lanes school contributions

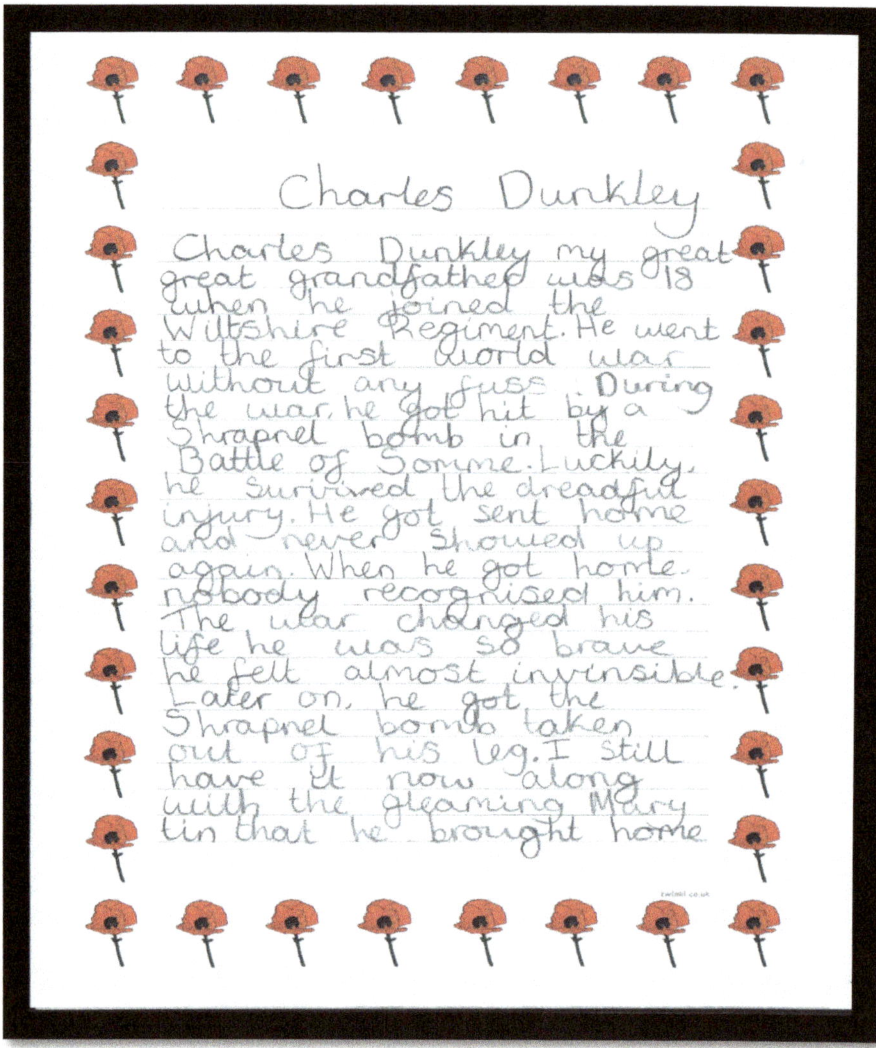

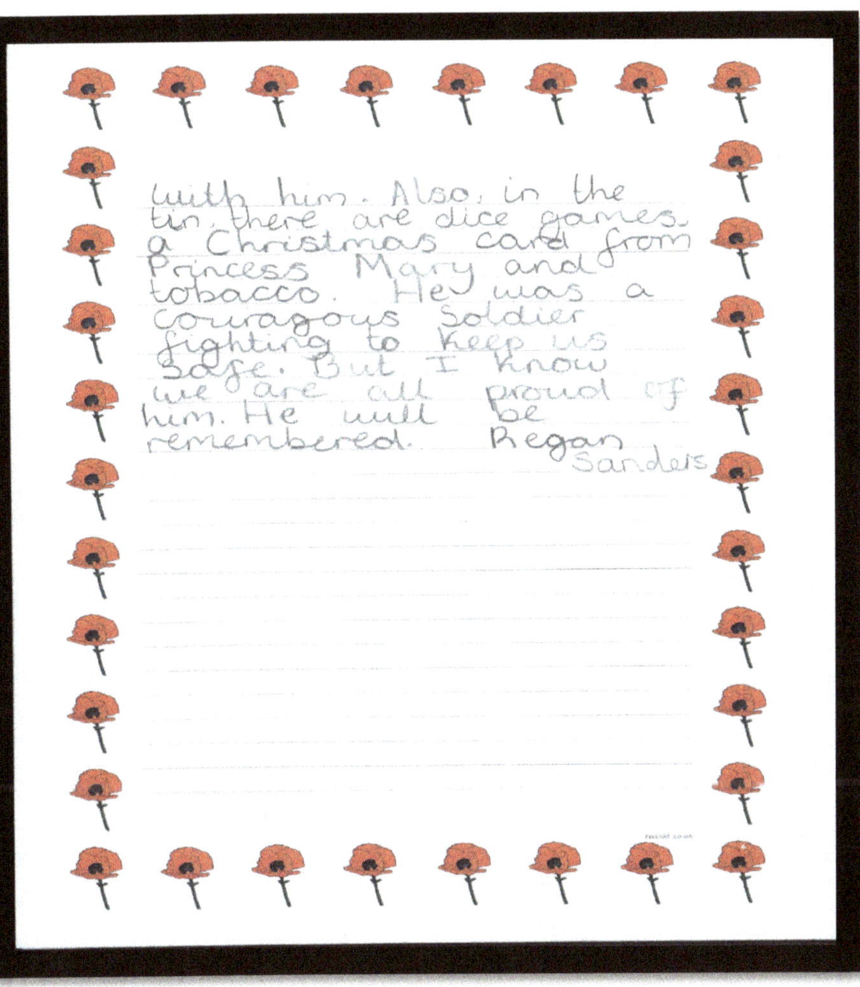
with him. Also, in the tin, there are dice games, a Christmas card from Princess Mary and tobacco. He was a couragous Soldier fighting to keep us safe. But I know we are all proud of him. He will be remembered. Regan Sanders

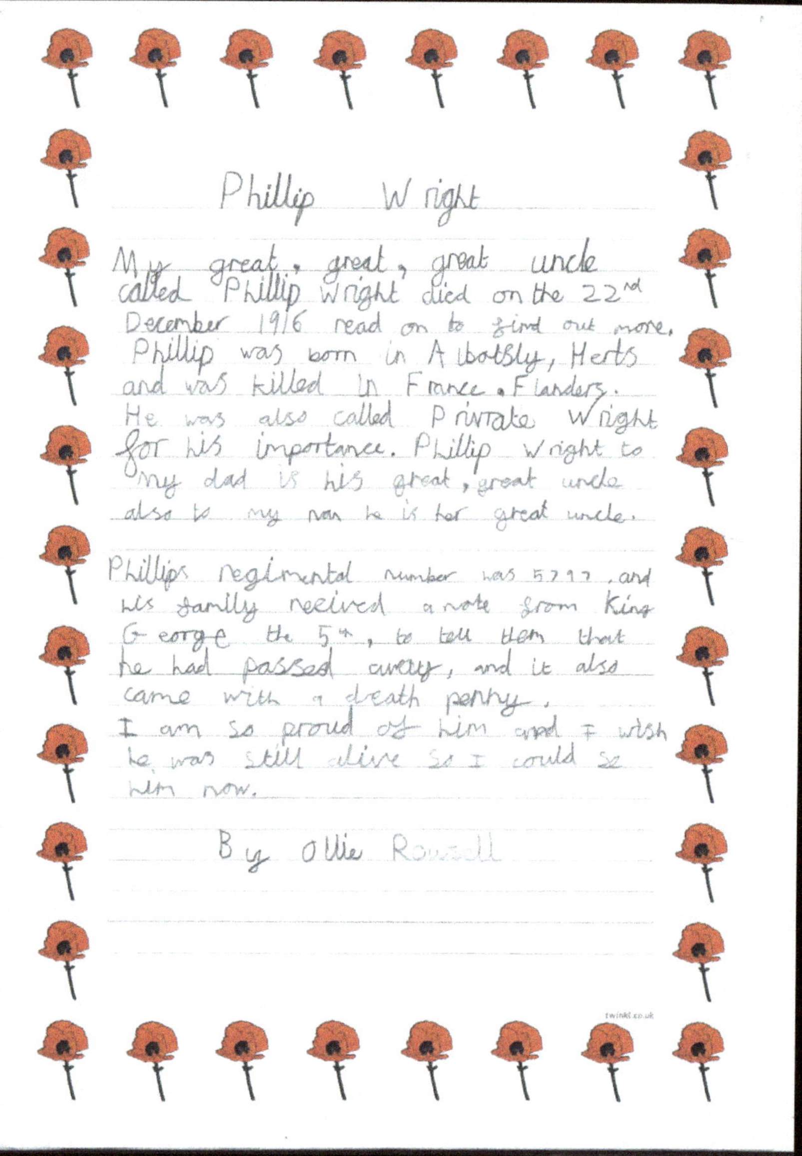

Phillip Wright

My great, great, great uncle called Phillip Wright died on the 22nd December 1916 read on to find out more. Phillip was born in Albotsly, Herts and was killed in France, Flanders. He was also called Private Wright for his importance. Phillip Wright to my dad is his great, great uncle also to my nan he is her great uncle.

Phillips regimental number was 5797, and his family recived a note from King George the 5th, to tell them that he had passed away, and it also came with a death penny.
I am so proud of him and I wish he was still alive so I could se him now.

By Ollie Rowell

twinkl.co.uk

2

battle was happening. A few weeks back I discovered that he was badly wounded not once but twice at Abbeville once in the chest and another in the face. He was extremely lucky that he lived after being transferred to hospital back in England.

I have a very insperational family because not only did William fight in the war but his son fought in World war 2. Lindsey Essex was his name and he was a gunner in the RAF (Royal Air Force). Lindsey's wife was in the Womans Land Army, these incredible woman played a massive part during the war. Her name was Esther Wren, whose father Charles Wren fought alongside many other brave soldiers in World War I. He was part of the fantastic Essex Regimant. He always walked with a limp due to shrapnel in his leg later having it amputated and getting a wodden

Jess

twinkl.co.uk

3

leg.

My Mums Grandad (Alfred Ford) worked with the horses he chose to do this because he was very passionate about horses despite his passion after seeing many unexcepted and dreadful things happened during the war, he never ever spoke about his experince again, i'm sure there were many people just like him.

My great great grandad was a brave heroic soldier who never gave up despite being injured many times. After the war, he decided to stay in England which changed my life today, however he truly missed his home. I think William Esser is a great inspiration for me and will remind me to keep strong minded.

Jess.
Worrow

twinkl.co.uk

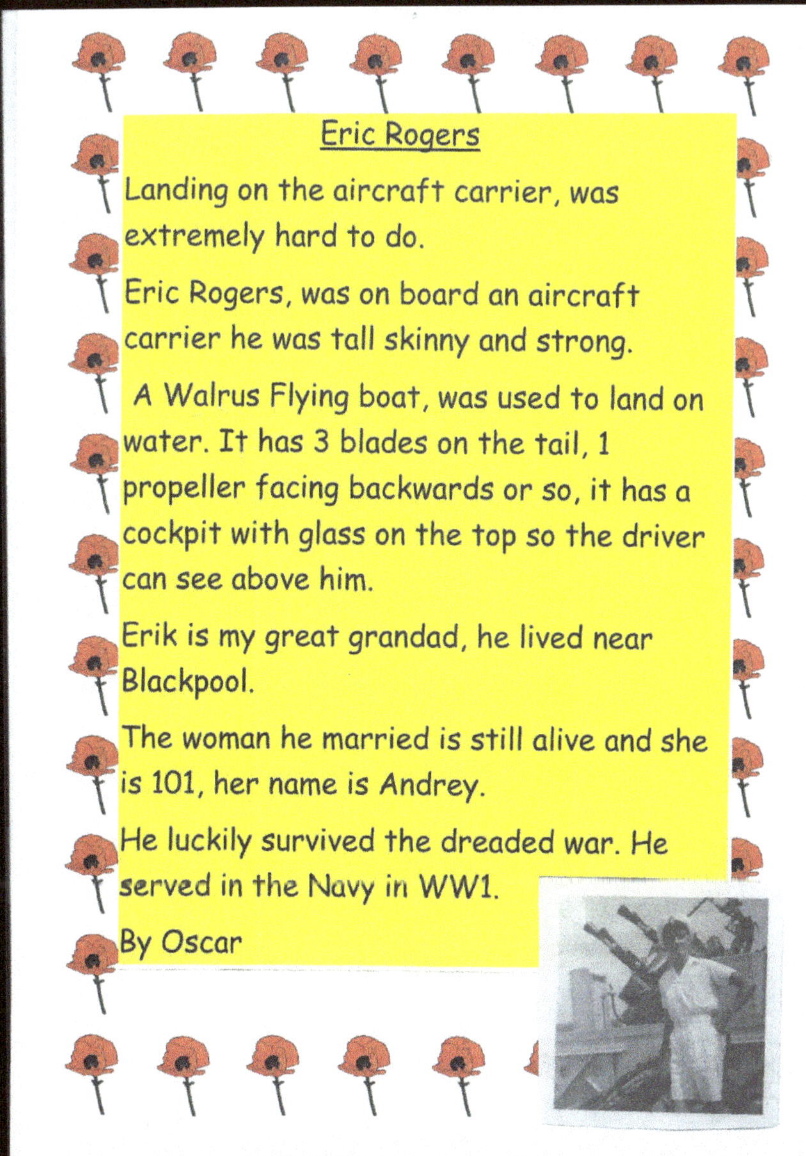

Eric Rogers

Landing on the aircraft carrier, was extremely hard to do.

Eric Rogers, was on board an aircraft carrier he was tall skinny and strong.

A Walrus Flying boat, was used to land on water. It has 3 blades on the tail, 1 propeller facing backwards or so, it has a cockpit with glass on the top so the driver can see above him.

Erik is my great grandad, he lived near Blackpool.

The woman he married is still alive and she is 101, her name is Andrey.

He luckily survived the dreaded war. He served in the Navy in WW1.

By Oscar

THE EVENT IN PICTURES

BRITONS
YOU
JOIN YOUR COUNTRY'S ARMY!
GOD SAVE THE KING

Daily Mail

ALLIED TROOPS TAKE CAMBRAI

Most important town yet as German soldiers flee the front

PREMIER'S DELIGHT AT 'SIGNIFICANT SUCCESS'

GERMOLENE
–the Magic Healer

Wilson refuses German peace offer

ROBBIALAC PAINTS PROTECT PROPERTY

Daily Mail

++ New Chancellor contacts Wilson ++ Hun army in full retreat ++ Britain is clear: We won't negotiate with Kaiser

GERMANY ASKS THE ALLIES FOR PEACE

SOLIDOX

The Star

LUNCH EDN.

The Eleventh Hour!

NEW PEACE DELEGATES ON THE WAY.

GERMANY FOLLOWS RUSSIA.

EXTENSION MAY BE ASKED.

Daily Mail

GREAT BREAKTHROUGH AT AMIENS

Lloyd George: 'Germany has lost her chance'

NINE MILES GAINED AT FARTHEST POINT

WHITELEYS
300 Baby Carriages

Advance has the Hun on the run

1918-2018
WE WILL
REMEMBER
THEM

www.ingramcontent.com/pod-product-compliance
Ingram Content Group UK Ltd.
Pitfield, Milton Keynes, MK11 3LW, UK
UKHW062313290726
14090UKWH00018B/1051

9 781789 558067